BAXTER
THEATRE
CENTRE
at the UNIVERSITY OF CAPE TOWN

Main Road, Rondebosch, Cape Town, South Africa
PO Box 297, Rondebosch, 7701
Tel: + 27 21 685 7880
www.baxter.co.za
facebook.com/BaxterTheatre
twitter.com/BaxterTheatre

THE FALL

produced by the Baxter Theatre Centre
at the University of Cape Town

CAST

Qhawekazi (The Brave One) **Tankiso Mamabolo**
Zukile-Libalele (The Wounded One) **Sihle Mnqwazana**
Camilla (The One Who Searches) **Ameera Conrad**
Kgothatso (The One Who Discovers) **Oarabile Ditsele**
Cahya (The Light) **Cleo Raatus**
Chwaita (The Young One) **Zandile Madliwa**
Boitshoko (The One Who Perseveres) **Sizwesandile Mnisi**

Written by	Ameera Conrad, Cleo Raatus, Kgomotso Khunoane, Oarabile Ditsele, Sihle Mnqwazana, Sizwesandile Mnisi, Tankiso Mamabolo and Thando Mangcu
Curated by	Ameera Conrad and Thando Mangcu
Facilitated by	Clare Stopford
Lighting Design	Luyanda Somkhence
Executive Producer	Lara Foot
Set Design	Patrick Curtis
Costume Design	Marisa Steenkamp

BAXTER THEATRE CENTRE
at the UNIVERSITY OF CAPE TOWN

PRODUCTION HISTORY

October 2016 – Golden Arrow Studio, Baxter Theatre Centre
January 2017 – Solution Space, Philippi Village
March 2017 – Cloetesville High School, Stellenbosch:
Woordfees
June 2017 – Golden Arrow Studio, Baxter Theatre Centre
August 2017 – Edinburgh Assembly Fringe Festival, Scotland
September 2017 – Golden Arrow Studio, Baxter Theatre Centre
September/October 2017 – The Royal Court Theatre, London

AWARDS

The Encore Award, Fleur du Cap Theatre Awards, 2017

The Stage Cast Award, Edinburgh Festival, 2017

The Scotsman Fringe First Award, Edinburgh Festival, 2017

Shortlisted for Amnesty International Freedom of Expression
Award, 2017

SPONSORS

THE COMPANY

Ameera Conrad (Camilla)

Ameera Conrad was born in Cape Town, and graduated with distinction from the University of Cape Town's Drama Department in 2015 as a Theatre Maker (Honours). In her final year, she co-wrote and starred in the UCT Grahamstown National Arts Festival production, *Don't Shoot the Harbinger* (Winner: Best New Script), and wrote, directed and performed live voice-overs in her graduating production, *bloom.*

Outside of the theatre world, Ameera has also been published in the UCT *SAX Appeal* (Dear White Boys™), the *Cape Argus* and *Mahala* magazine.

Professionally, Ameera has found success as a writer, director, and performer. In 2016 she wrote a short play for Anthology: *Young Bloods* (directed by Louis Viljoen at the Alexander Bar), performed in and co-curated *The Fall* at the Baxter Theatre, and was one of the recipients of the 2016 Theatre Arts Admin Collective's Emerging Theatre Director's Bursary, where she directed her self-written piece *Reparation*, which will be published in 2017 by Junkets.

Cleo Raatus (Cahya)

Cleo Raatus is an actor, singer, theatre-maker and producer who graduated at the top of his acting class at the University of Cape Town in 2015 with a BA (Hons) in Theatre and Performance. In his final year, he performed in *Black Dog/Inj'emnyama*, directed by Clare Stopford; and performed a cabaret curated with Tankiso Mamabolo at the Voorkamerfees at the end of his final year.

Raatus had his professional theatre debut in *District Six: Kanala* in early 2016 and returned for three seasons. He went on to curate and perform in *Some Days* alongside Tankiso Mamabolo and Sizwesandile Mnisi before the premiere of *The Fall*.

In 2016–17 Raatus reprised his role in *District Six: Kanala*, and played in Howard Barker's *Scenes from an Execution* and Jon Keevy's *The Underground Library*.

Oarabile Ditsele (Kgothatso)

Oarabile Ditsele is an actor, theatre-maker, writer and producer who believes in the documenting of stories of young people as they live them. Oarabile has performed in South Africa and around Africa, spreading a message of empowerment. His debut into theatre, after graduating from the University of Cape Town with a BA (Hons) in Theatre & Performance was *Woza Albert!*, directed by Fleur du Cap Award-winning director Mdu Kweyama. He later went on to be involved in creating and performing in Fleur du Cap Award-winning play, *The Fall*. He played Fabian in *Twelfth Night* at the Maynardville Open-Air Theatre in 2017.

'Tsela kgopo ga e ya latsa nageng.'

Sihle Mnqwazana (Zukile-Libalele)

Born in 1993 in the informal settlement of Bekkersdal, Sihle Mnqwazana was raised by a single mother in a family of seven, with two siblings, three cousins and an aunt. He grew up between Westonaria, a former mining town, and the village of Ngolo in Mthatha. After matric he went on to study Theatre and Performance at the University of Cape Town, where he obtained a BA (Hons) degree in 2015. He has since performed on numerous theatre stages, both locally and internationally.

He starred in two short films which have been screened at the 48 Hour Film Festival and the Kleinkaap Short Film Festival. He also features in the international pilot, *Rise of the Phoenix*, directed by Nic Franklin and Mark Dymond.

In 2016 he made the top six of the highly acclaimed Brett Goldin Bursary, a great achievement that attests to the versatility of this young actor. He has since performed in three professional productions: Athol Fugard's *My Children! My Africa!*, directed by Mahlatsi Mokgonyana (Theatre Arts Admin); *Identirrhaging*, written & directed by Nwabisa Plaatjie (Rosebank Theatre); *Connection to home*, devised and directed by the cast, in collaboration with Metrics Productions (Gorèe Diaspora Festival).

In addition, the 23-year-old is among the founders of Age of the Artist, which is an active movement of free-thinkers in multidisciplinary fields committed to creating art that is both accessible and self-sufficient.

When he is not on stage or on set, writing scripts and conference papers, Sihle helps out as a Nal'ibali ambassador at libraries and communities around the Western Cape and his home town of Westonaria.

Sizwesandile Mnisi (Boitshoko)

Sizwesandile Mnisi is a Motswana actor, singer, and a dancer. He is also a director, writer and choreographer, born in Pretoria and raised in Hammanskraal where he learnt to find his own authentic voice as a young black man. He left Pretoria for Cape Town after his matric year to further his studies and chase his dreams.

Since his graduation at the University of Cape Town's drama school in 2015, Sizwe has been working both in the theatre and in film, performing in Germany and Senegal. He directed the physical theatre play, *Monna Ga Se Nku*, performed and produced by Baikitsi Arts Collective (a black-owned theatre company and production house he co-founded in 2014). He was in *Woza Albert!* at the Baxter Theatre in 2016, directed by Fleur du Cap Award-winning director, Mdu Kweyama – the run was extended by popular demand. He is part of the cast of the second season of *Our Girl*, a BBC series directed by Jan Matthys. Sizwe also performed in Nwabisa Plaatjie's *Identirrhaging*, produced by Age of the Artist for 2016 Youth Month. Sizwe's work is set around Afrocentrism and seeks to challenge representations of black masculinity.

Zandile Madliwa (Chwaita)

Zandile Madliwa studied BA Theatre and Performance at UCT. The 25-year-old actress and vocalist has, since graduating in 2015, performed on stage, television and in feature movies. Her first professional acting job was as the lead character in SABC's *When We Were Black 2*. In 2016 she went on an international tour in the USA where she played Miriam Makeba's daughter, Bongi Makeba, in the musical *Mama Afrika*. Her film credits include *On the Ropes* and *The Kissing Booth*. She has also appeared on the Netflix series *Black Mirror* and the KykNet series *Die Boekklub* and she has performed at the Market Theatre in the musical show *Songs fom Jazztown*. Zandile joined *The Fall* cast for its season at the 2017 Edinburgh Assembly Fringe Festival.

Tankiso Mamabolo (Qhawekazi)

Tankiso Mamabolo is a passionate singer, actress and dancer from Mthatha in the Eastern Cape. She graduated from the University of Cape Town in 2015 with a BA (Hons) in Theatre and Performance.

Tankiso's journey began in 2011 when she won the Arts and Culture Trust performing arts scholarship. Since then she has embarked on many artistic journeys, including *Titus Andronicus*, directed by Geoffrey Hyland, and *'BackDog'/ Inj'emnyama* at The Baxter Theatre, directed by Clare Stopford. In 2013 she performed alongside Gloria Bosman and Kate Normington at the annual Arts and Culture Awards and a year later performed in a musical cabaret alongside Cleo Raatus (*District Six: Kanala*) at the Voorkamerfees.

In 2016 she performed in *Die Van Aardes van Grootoor: the musical* at the Theatre on The Bay, directed by Peter-Dirk Uys and Godfrey Johnson. She was part of the first ever John Kani season at the Artscape Theatre, where she played Thando in *Nothing but the Truth*, directed by John Kani. She has also worked on *Some Days*, a musical revue performed with Sizwesandile Mnisi and Cleo Raatus at the Alexander Bar theatre.

Her most recent work includes *The Fall* and *Marat/Sade*, directed by the award-winning Jaco Bouwer at the Baxter Theatre.

Thando Mangcu (Chwaita / Curator)

Thando Mangcu was born in Elmira, New York, in 1993. Most of her childhood was spent in Johannesburg; she attended St Stithians Girls' College where she trained in classical piano and saxophone. Her Black Radical Feminism is attributed to her mother, Phelisa, who (with her close network of womxn friends) later raised her and her sisters as a single parent.

In her final university year she created *Luderitz* and *The Credit Gone Away Affair* (an adaptation of Alain Mabanckou's *Broken Glass*). She co-wrote (along with Ameera Conrad and Katya Mendelson) *Don't Shoot the Harbinger*, which won the Most Promising Writer's award at the 2015 National Arts Festival.

Her current interests are in site-specific and avant-garde performance, focusing on materials and image. This she has pursued by performing at the ICA (formerly GIPCA) Live Art Festival (2014) and in subsequently shadowing Sello Pesa of Ntsoana Contemporary Theatre and their site-specific work. She has co-choreographed with Sizwesandile Mnisi and Sihle Mnqwazana *Delayed Replays* (2017).

Her film acting includes *Confrontation*, written by Stephanie Dadet and directed by Timothy Carlson as part of the international Our City Film Project (2017).

She is a graduate of UCT Drama School with a BA (Hons) in Theatre and Performance, specialising in Theatre Making. She is also a founding member of the network, Age of the Artist.

THE BAXTER THEATRE CENTRE

On 1 August 2017, the Baxter Theatre Centre celebrated its 40th anniversary. To mark this milestone, the iconic theatre embarked on an exciting and innovative initiative called the 40/80 Campaign. A simple and accessible fundraising drive was launched by inviting the public and the business sector to join the theatre to turn a 40-year legacy into an 80-year commitment, thereby, ensuring that this illustrious legacy will continue for future audiences and artists.

Designed by the award-winning architect Jack Barnett, the theatre came into being as the result of a bequest from the late Dr William Duncan Baxter who, in his will, bequeathed a sum of money to the University of Cape Town (UCT) for the purpose of establishing a theatre which would, in his words, "develop and cultivate the arts in Cape Town and the adjacent districts for all artists". This bequest was split between building the premises and establishing a permanent endowment fund for the Baxter's activities.

Barnett wanted to design a theatre that embodied the South African spirit and culture, at a time when South Africa was much divided. A theatre like the Baxter had to embrace all the people of Cape Town, which was difficult due to the laws that were enforced in the country at the time. The Entertainment Act of 1931 introduced legal censorship and the Publication and Entertainment Act of 1963 segregated black and white audiences, unless under special licences. To build the Baxter in the city centre meant that people of colour couldn't access it and that is why the University of Cape Town (UCT) became a strategic location for a theatre for all.

At the forefront of the performing arts, both as a popular venue and as a leading award-winning producer, the Baxter presents cutting edge works and masterpieces from local and international repertoires. Since its inception the theatre has stayed true to its promise of always being open to everyone who visit it and to create work of the highest artistic quality. The objective is to reflect the cultures of all the people of South Africa on its stages and in its foyers and galleries and, thereby, nurturing an interactive and meaningful relationship with its audiences and patrons, while generating a spirit of goodwill and creativity.

The Baxter does not receive any funding from the national government or from the National Lotteries Commission. It is not considered a state entity and is not eligible for funding, and for the past 10 years the Lottery has denied funding due to its association with UCT. However, UCT covers approximately 40% of the Baxter's operational costs and the balance of 60% has to be raised by the theatre.

Despite these limitations the Baxter Theatre Centre has become widely regarded as one of the premier theatres in the country - winning awards and receiving accolades and recognition for its inherent and proudly South African productions which speak to the heart of the country's social landscape with universal themes.

To find out more about the Baxter's 40/80 Campaign
or how to support the theatre
visit **www.baxter.co.za**

LARA FOOT, CEO AND ARTISTIC DIRECTOR OF BAXTER THEATRE CENTRE
AND EXECUTIVE PRODUCER OF *THE FALL*

Since being appointed as the first female CEO and Artistic Director of the Baxter Theatre Centre in January 2010, Lara Foot, through her vision, has given further meaning to the legacy and mission of the award-winning theatre.

Foot is a multi-award-winning playwright, director and producer; a former Rolex protégé to the late Sir Peter Hall in the prestigious Rolex Mentor and Protégé programme, as well as a Sundance Fellow.

In August 2017, as executive producer, she achieved the rare distinction of taking six Baxter productions, comprising a team of 30 actors and crew, to the 2017 Edinburgh Festival Fringe. The South African season comprised *The Fall*, Lara Foot's *Tshepang: The Third Testament*, *Karoo Moose – No Fathers* and *The Inconvenience of Wings*, Sylvaine Strike's *Tobacco* and Yael Farber's *Mies Julie*. Each of these productions received at least one (and in some cases more) five-star reviews and standing ovations in Edinburgh. *The Fall* received *The Scotsman* Fringe First Award which celebrates the best new writing, and *The Stage* Edinburgh Acting Award for the ensemble for their performances. The production was also shortlisted for the Amnesty International Freedom of Expression Award.

With a passion for the development of new indigenous work, young writers and directors, Lara has put most of her energy into helping playwrights and theatre-makers realise their work, having nurtured several dozen new South African plays to their first staging. She has directed over 50 professional productions, 38 of which have been new South African plays.

Together with a dynamic team, she has transformed the Baxter's hugely successful development programme – the Zabalaza Theatre Festival – to become recognised and respected as one of the most vital and important platforms of its kind in South Africa. As a former Rolex protégé, she hosted a unique cultural gathering at the Baxter with renowned Mentors William Kentridge, Wole Soyinka and Peter Sellars, alongside seven protégés.

In 2016 Lara was the Featured Artist at the 43rd National Arts Festival, leading the charge on the Main Programme which is made up of 80% of work written, directed, curated or headlined by women. This, two decades after she was selected as the Standard Young Artist for Drama. With a host of South African theatre accolades to her name, her own hard-hitting plays tackle social issues in South Africa and these have earned her great respect and recognition locally and internationally.

Tshepang, *Hear And Now*, *Reach*, *Karoo Moose*, *Solomon and Marion* (all published by Oberon Books), *Fishers of Hope* and *The Inconvenience of Wings* are just a few of her plays which have won multiple awards and that have toured internationally with great success. *Fishers of Hope* scooped four awards at the Naledi Theatre Awards in Johannesburg, including the coveted Best Production of a Play accolade. Earlier this year her latest play, *The Inconvenience of Wings*, earned her the Best Director honour, along with the Best Actress (Jenifer Steyn) and Best Actor (Andrew Buckland) nods at the 2017 Fleur du Cap awards. She also clinched three awards (Best Director, Best Production of a Play and Best Actress), for her play *Karoo Moose* at the 2017 Klein Karoo National Arts Festival (the largest Afrikaans Festival in South Africa).

Picture: Baxter Theatre Centre, interior

THE ROYAL COURT THEATRE

The Royal Court Theatre is the writers' theatre. It is a leading force in world theatre for energetically cultivating writers – undiscovered, emerging and established.

Through the writers, the Royal Court is at the forefront of creating restless, alert, provocative theatre about now. We open our doors to the unheard voices and free thinkers that, through their writing, change our way of seeing.

Over 120,000 people visit the Royal Court in Sloane Square, London, each year and many thousands more see our work elsewhere through transfers to the West End and New York, UK and international tours, digital platforms, our residencies across London, and our site-specific work. Through all our work we strive to inspire audiences and influence future writers with radical thinking and provocative discussion.

The Royal Court's extensive development activity encompasses a diverse range of writers and artists and includes an ongoing programme of writers' attachments, readings, workshops and playwriting groups. Twenty years of the International Department's pioneering work around the world means the Royal Court has relationships with writers on every continent.

Within the past sixty years, John Osborne, Samuel Beckett, Arnold Wesker, Ann Jellicoe, Howard Brenton and David Hare have started their careers at the Court. Many others including Caryl Churchill, Athol Fugard, Mark Ravenhill, Simon Stephens, debbie tucker green, Sarah Kane – and, more recently, Lucy Kirkwood, Nick Payne, Penelope Skinner and Alistair McDowall – have followed.

The Royal Court has produced many iconic plays from Laura Wade's **Posh** to Jez Butterworth's **Jerusalem** and Martin McDonagh's **Hangmen**.

Royal Court plays from every decade are now performed on stage and taught in classrooms and universities across the globe.

It is because of this commitment to the writer that we believe there is no more important theatre in the world than the Royal Court.

Supported using public funding by
ARTS COUNCIL ENGLAND

NTERNATIONAL PLAYWRIGHTS
T THE ROYAL COURT THEATRE

ver the last two decades the Royal Court Theatre has led the way in the development and oduction of new international plays, facilitating work at grass-roots level and developing changes which brings UK writers and directors to work with emerging artists around the orld. Through a programme of long-term workshops and residencies, in London and abroad, a eative dialogue now exists with theatre practitioners from over 70 countries, working in over languages, most recently Argentina, Chile, China, Cuba, Georgia, India, Lebanon, Mexico, lestine, Russia, South Africa, Syria, Turkey, Ukraine, Uruguay and Zimbabwe. All of these velopment projects are supported by the Genesis Foundation and the British Council.

e Royal Court Theatre has produced dozens of new international plays through this ogramme since 1997, most recently **B** by Guillermo Calderón (Chile), **I See You** by ngiwekhaya (South Africa), **Fireworks** by Dalia Taha (Palestine), **The Djinns of Eidgah** Abhishek Majumdar (India), **A Time to Reap** by Anna Wakulik (Poland), **Remembrance ay** by Aleksey Scherbak (Latvia), **Our Private Life** by Pedro Miguel Rozo (Colombia), and **sconnect** by Anupama Chandrasekhar (India).

o new international plays that have come through this development process will be produced er this year: **Bad Roads** by Natal'ya Vorozhbit (Ukraine) and **Goats** by Liwaa Yazji (Syria).

)YAL COURT AND SOUTH AFRICA

e Royal Court has a longstanding connection to new writing in South Africa. In 1973, **Sizwe nzi is Dead** by Athol Fugard, John Kani and Winston Ntshona was produced in the rwood Theatre Upstairs and was followed by a season of three plays in the Jerwood Theatre wnstairs. John Kani described the Court at that time as his home: "To find a theatre in the e world with the same kind of vision gave us so much hope that the world was aware of our ffering." In July 2014, exactly 40 years later a new project was born in a new South Africa. elve young writers from all parts of the country were selected to take part in a two year oject, working with playwrights Leo Butler, Winsome Pinnock and International Director 'se Dodgson supported by the British Council and Connect ZA. As a result eleven new ys for South Africa and the world were created – works that gave us an insight into South ican life today and the urgent concerns of a younger generation two decades after the end apartheid. In May 2014 six of the writers were invited to London to present their work as ged readings **New Plays from South Africa: After 20 Years**. In 2015 the Market eatre in Johannesburg staged readings of all eleven plays and many of them have now had productions in some of the country's major theatres. The writers have formed a powerful lective to support new writing in South Africa, Play Riot, and **I See You** by Mongikewaya, ected by Noma Dumezweni, was produced in the Jerwood Theatre Upstairs in March 2016. As first co-production between the Royal Court and the Market Theatre this was followed by a at the Fugard Theatre in Cape Town and many national awards which include: The Fleur du p Award for Best New South African Script and the Naledi Theatre Award for Best Production d Best Actor.

ROYAL COURT SUPPORTERS

The Royal Court is a registered charity and not-for-profit company. Our supporters enable us to remain the write theatre, find stories from everywhere and create theatre for everyone. Thank you, we can't do it without you.

PUBLIC FUNDING

Arts Council England,
London
British Council

TRUSTS & FOUNDATIONS

The Bryan Adams
Charitable Trust
The Austin & Hope
Pilkington Trust
Martin Bowley Charitable
Trust
Gerald Chapman Fund
CHK Charities
The City Bridge Trust
The Clifford Chance
Foundation
Cockayne - Grants for the
Arts
The Noel Coward
Foundation
Cowley Charitable Trust
The Eranda Rothschild
Foundation
Lady Antonia Fraser for
The Pinter Commission
Genesis Foundation
The Golden Bottle Trust
The Haberdashers'
Company
The Paul Hamlyn
Foundation
Roderick & Elizabeth
Jack
Jerwood Charitable
Foundation
Kirsh Foundation
The Mackintosh
Foundation
The Andrew Lloyd
Webber Foundation
The London Community
Foundation
John Lyon's Charity
Clare McIntyre's Bursary
The David & Elaine Potter
Foundation
The Richard Radcliffe
Charitable Trust
Rose Foundation
Royal Victoria Hall
Foundation
The Sackler Trust
The Sobell Foundation
John Thaw Foundation
The Garfield Weston
Foundation

CORPORATE SPONSORS

Aqua Financial Solutions
Ltd
Bloomberg
Cadogan Estates
Colbert
Edwardian Hotels, London
Fever-Tree
Gedye & Sons
Kirkland & Ellis
International LLP
Kudos
MAC
Room One
Sister Pictures
Sky Drama

BUSINESS MEMBERS

Annoushka Jewellery
Auerbach & Steele
Opticians
CNC – Communications &
Network Consulting
Cream
Lansons
Left Bank Pictures
Rockspring Property
Investment Managers
Tetragon Financial Group

INDIVIDUAL SUPPORTERS

Artistic Director's Circle

Eric Abraham
Carolyn Bennett
Samantha & Richard
Campbell-Breeden
Cas Donald
Lydia & Manfred Gorvy
Charles Holloway
Luke Johnson
Jack & Linda Keenan
Angelie & Shafin Moledina
Miles Morland
Anatol Orient
NoraLee & Jon Sedmak
Deborah Shaw
& Stephen Marquardt
Jan & Michael Topham
Matthew & Sian
Westerman
Mahdi Yahya

Writers' Circle

Mark & Charlotte
Cunningham
Scott M Delman
Jane Featherstone
Piers & Melanie Gibson
Jean & David Grier

Mandeep Manku
Emma O'Donoghue
Mr & Mrs Sandy Orr
Carol Sellars
Maureen & Tony Wheeler
The Wilhelm Helmut Trust
Anonymous

Directors' Circle

William & Asli Arah
Dr Kate Best
Katie Bradford
Piers Butler
Chris & Alison Cabot
Emma & Phil Coffer
Joachim Fleury
Louis Greig
David & Claudia Harding
Roderick & Elizabeth
Jack
Melanie J Johnson
Nicola Kerr
Mrs Joan Kingsley
Emma Marsh
Rachel Mason
Andrew & Ariana Rodger
Anonymous

Platinum Members

Moira Andreae
Nick Archdale
Elizabeth & Adam
Bandeen
Clive & Helena Butler
Gavin & Lesley Casey
Sarah & Philippe
Chappatte
Michael & Arlene Cohrs
Clyde Cooper
Mrs Lara Cross
T Cross
Andrew & Amanda Cryer
Shane & Catherine
Cullinane
Alison Davies
Matthew Dean
Sarah Denning
Cherry & Rob Dickins
Denise & Randolph
Dumas
Robyn Durie
Mark & Sarah Evans
Sally & Giles Everist
Celeste & Peter Fenichel
Emily Fletcher
The Edwin Fox Foundation
Dominic & Claire
Freemantle
Beverley Gee
Nick & Julie Gould
The Richard Grand
Foundation
Jill Hackel & Andrzej
Zarzycki

Carol Hall
Peter & Debbie
Hargreaves
Sam & Caroline Haubold
Mr & Mrs Gordon Holmes
Dr Timothy Hyde
Damien Hyland
Trevor Ingman
Amanda & Chris Jennings
Ralph Kanter
David P Kaskel
& Christopher A Teano
Vincent & Amanda
Keaveny
Peter & Maria Kellner
Mr & Mrs Pawel
Kisielewski
Rosemary Leith
Kathryn Ludlow
The Maplescombe Trust
Christopher Marek
Rencki
Mrs Janet Martin
Andrew McIver
David & Elizabeth Miles
David Mills
Barbara Minto
M.E. Murphy Altschuler
Siobhan Murphy
Peter & Maggie
Murray-Smith
Georgia Oetker
Adam Oliver-Watkins
Crispin Osborne
Alexander Petalas
Andrea & Hilary Ponti
Theo Priovolos
Greg & Karen Reid
Paul & Gill Robinson
Corinne Rooney
Sir Paul & Lady Ruddock
William & Hilary Russell
Sally & Anthony Salz
Antoinette Santamaria
Jane Scobie
Anita Scott
Bhags Sharma
Dr. Wendy Sigle
Andy Simpkin
Brian Smith
Mr John Soler & Meg
Morrison
Maria Sukkar
Kim Taylor-Smith
Mrs Caroline Thomas
Alex Timken
The Ulrich Family
Monica B Voldstad
Arrelle & François Von
Hurter
Anne-Marie Williams
Sir Robert & Lady Wilson
Anonymous

THE FALL

devised by

Ameera Conrad
Cleo Raatus
Kgomotso Khunoane
Oarabile Ditsele
Sihle Mnqwazana
Sizwesandile Mnisi
Tankiso Mamabolo
Thando Mangcu

OBERON BOOKS
LONDON

WWW.OBERONBOOKS.COM

First published in 2017 by Junkets Publisher
PO Box 38040, Pinelands, 7430, South Africa
email: info.junkets@iafrica.com
www.junkets.co.za

First published in the UK in 2017 by Oberon Books Ltd
521 Caledonian Road, London N7 9RH
Tel: +44 (0) 20 7607 3637 / Fax: +44 (0) 20 7607 3629
e-mail: info@oberonbooks.com
www.oberonbooks.com

A catalogue record for this book is available from the British Library.

PB ISBN: 9781786823625
E ISBN: 9781786823632

Cover and photography by Oscar O'Ryan

Printed and bound by 4edge Limited, Essex, UK.
eBook conversion by CPI Group (UK) Ltd, Croydon, CR0 4YY.

Visit www.oberonbooks.com to read more about all our books and to buy them. You will also find features, author interviews and news of any author events, and you can sign up for e-newsletters so that you're always first to hear about our new releases.

PRAISE FOR *THE FALL*

This is history told just as it happens.
— Siya Mahomba, *What's on in Cape Town*

The revolution may not be televised, it is definitely being staged.
— Tracey Saunders, *IOL*

… an insightful must for anyone who wants to understand just what the students are thinking and why things have turned violent.
— Theresa Smith, *Cape Argus*

There is no doubt that this work is full-throated, full-throttle, militantly artistic theatre – on stage and page.
— Adrienne Sichel, *Cape Times*

Singing truth to power… Each individual is a frighteningly good actor… There surely cannot be a better cast at the Fringe this year.
— *All Edinburgh Theatre*, ★★★★★

We dedicate this to all the students and workers who marched for free, decolonial education.

AUTHORS' NOTE

Currently, colonisation continues to haunt us materially, socially and psychologically. Students, workers and academics all over South Africa are taking it upon themselves to tackle the continuing, silent, traumatic effects of oppression in South Africa.

The #RhodesMustFall Movement served as a major clarion call to a mass of people of colour at the University of Cape Town (UCT) and tertiary institutions all over South Africa. Although there were working groups long before the famous 'poo-throwing', the mass student movement (and the ones that followed throughout the year, all over the country) provoked worldwide discourse and action. The movement ballooned into wider discussion on Blackness, feminism, institutionalised racism, sexuality, transgender and gender non-binary erasure. The movement highlighted the conversation about access to education, as well as in decolonising the colonial structures within the education system.

Students all over South Africa had been articulating and trying to resolve what many had been thinking and feeling before. Equality and justice cannot only be served through legislation. Trauma is rooted in the everyday experiences of the oppressed.

The Fall is a collaborative piece of Workshop Theatre devised by eight former students, some of whom were involved and some affected by the movement in different ways. The writing and rehearsal process was facilitated by director and UCT lecturer Clare Stopford. The play is based on the writers' experiences as people of colour during the #RhodesMustFall and subsequent movements. The play is written solely from the students' perspectives and homes in on their individual and intersectional challenges in the movement.

The project started after the 2015 run of *Black Dog* (workshopped by the original cast) at the Baxter Theatre. The challenge of telling the story of students in the 1976 uprisings invited the idea of reflecting lives of People of Colour forty years from 1976 – as ourselves.

The Fall thus came as a reply to and follow-up of *Black Dog*, but simultaneously as a retrospective gaze and reflection on the events after the #RhodesMustFall Movement started – most importantly, from the perspectives of students of colour.

The play doesn't offer solutions but it hopes to raise dialogue – as it did during the workshop process – on intersectional, institutionalised discrimination against the marginalised majority.

Please note: while the play has been scripted partially from the experiences of the actors, the characters and some of the events are fictional representations drawn from archives and research.

THANKS

Thank you to the staff of the Baxter Theatre – everyone from Lara Foot and the production team to the bartenders and Front of House. It is very rare for a young company of actors and theatre makers to be given a home and a safe space in which to create work, stretch our wings, and push some buttons. We would also like to thank Dr Pumla Gobodo Madikizela and the Mellon Foundation for their continued support and contribution to making the show a possibility.

Thank you to Clare Stopford for initiating this process and helping us to unpack our own thoughts and opinions and feelings around what was a very difficult and, in some instances, traumatic process. To the Drama Department at UCT and our lecturers there, thank you for seeing our individual talents and teaching us how to harness them for the best possible results.

Thank you to the audiences who came to support the show. For a production to have sold-out shows in its first run is unprecedented and we are so grateful to the people who came to watch us tell our stories. Thank you to our families and partners for their continued support, and of course, to God for allowing this path to open for us and for being with us every step of the way.

Theatre is important. Theatre has the most amazing ability to give people an understanding of what can often be very complex social issues by telling human stories, while at the same time speaking truth to power.

That is what we as the cast feel our duty is: to tell our stories. The call from students for decolonised education is a call that we stand behind entirely, and one that we believe should extend into all sectors, most especially the theatre.

And that is why we would like, lastly and most importantly, to thank all of the artists of colour who continue to make work that is inspiring and important; we see you and we are honoured to work among you.

Thank you.

SCENE 1: THE STORMING OF BREMNER

Empty stage. The surfaces of the set (walls and floor) are textured with a wallpaper of multiple, enlarged hashtags. Three tables are set up at the back, almost unnoticeable. They will be used to create different scenarios.

SONG: NOBODY WANNA SEE US TOGETHER.

ALL enter the stage as they sing and march in formation. The atmosphere is defiant and celebratory.

ZUKILE-LIBALELE: I will never forget that Friday, the 20th of March 2015. I remember marching next to my friend, uQhawekazi, holding up a cardboard poster that said, 'I march because Africa is all I have. Europe is not an option for me' – a statement that resonated with most of us at that march. We protested outside of UCT's administration building, iBremner. We stood in the heat for hours, singing and dancing, finding shade under our posters and trees. And then, a wave of bodies … sho!

CAHYA: We went from UCT students to uMkhonto weSizwe real fast. The VC was speaking on the mic but didn't give us the date when the statue would come down. So the mic was taken away from him and it was announced that we would march into Bremner administration building and occupy that space until management gave us the date. I didn't know whether to join in or wait outside. The problem was, as a member of the SRC I had to mediate between management and students. I waited for a moment and then I joined the wave.

QHAWEKAZI: Hai suka nina, I saw some of you standing in the shade with your expensive water-bottles. You see, for some of us, the falling of Rhodes would symbolise the falling of every colonial icon in this country, one by one. I remember, we marched into the Bremner foyer singing:

SONG: TLOSANG MAGWALA A CHE CHE.

BOITSHOKO: A song that calls the cowardly to stand aside for us – the bravehearts – to keep moving forward. And I'm telling you, we were brave.

CHWAITA: Ja, brave, but no respect for property! I was not about to be arrested alongside people who wanted to perpetuate the stereotype of the angry black.

BOITSHOKO: It was bloody hot inside the foyer and it didn't help that management deliberately switched off the fucking aircon system.

CHWAITA: But, yoh, I'd never seen so many people with such fire. I didn't know what to do, where to go, where I stood. I mean, to take the whole actual mic from the whole Vice Chancellor … then we pushed him aside!

CAMILLA: We were pushing against each other, sweating and singing, not knowing what would happen next. Fuck, man, it was historic! Finally, we were doing something. Finally, black students at UCT felt confident to speak about the traumas we face on this campus. We renamed Bremner building Azania House, a name given to South Africa by the PAC many years ago. It was there, at Azania House, that we began to share in each other's black pain.

KGOTHATSO: I remember thinking to myself: Bra! You don't storm buildings! I decided to let everyone go in first, because I didn't want them to call the police and then I get arrested with the first people who entered. Bru … I only entered that building later that afternoon.

The song builds.

CHWAITA: I heard someone was holding a gun!

The song pauses, and THE CAST grumble.

ZUKILE-LIBALELE: Suddenly, this was an occupation.

The song restarts.

ZUKILE-LIBALELE: We were starting our decolonial project and we were not going to leave until management had met all of our demands. Sithi phantsi ngo Rhodes phantsi!

ALL: Phantsi!

BOITSHOKO: Hey, mara, oGopole ge gore that occupation was carefully planned by the students. Guerrilla tactics, baba! We were prepared! Don't make it seem like we weren't prepared. Those gates were open. As far as I'm concerned, that was an invitation!

CAMILLA: Stop interrupting the story, man!

BOITSHOKO: Hayi, I was just saying. Don't make it seem like we did not anticipate the occupation.

QHAWEKAZI: Whatever. I remember, Prof. Mangcu, one of the black academics, he later met us in front of the Bremner foyer and there he commended us on our efforts. He said that the decolonial conversation we were starting was one that people like him have been pushing for years.

ALL: *Been* pushing!

ZUKILE-LIBALELE: … without recognition.

ALL: … mmm-m.

QHAWEKAZI: With their writings on philosophers and activists like Biko, Fanon …

CAHYA: Bell Hooks!

QHAWEKAZI: Bell Hooks!

CAMILLA: And Audre Lord.

QHAWEKAZI: Those names were to greatly influence the movement.

KGOTHATSO: We were not only determined to realise Biko's philosophy of black pride but we were also committed to becoming our own heroes by taking matters into our own hands. Late that afternoon we marched upstairs to the Mafeje Room.

SONG: BAZOSIBONA THINA.

KGOTHATSO: The building was erupting with song because we were occupying a space where management had made many executive decisions. Well, up until our occupation. We were becoming our own council, only accountable to the movement and its people.

Dancing and singing builds. THE CAST re-arrange the tables as they take over the room.

CHWAITA: I remember standing in the corner of the Mafeje Room, unable to sing or dance or speak. I mean, I'd never felt so many things at the same time before. All of these people looked so powerful and I was there feeling tiny and wanting to know what the rest of the world was thinking, seeing us dancing on top of the Vice Chancellor's tables!

Song stops.

QHAWEKAZI: No-no-no, Babes, those tables did not belong to the Vice Chancellor, they now belonged to the blacks. It was our turn to sit in meetings and decide the fate of the university.

Song continues.

CHWAITA: I heard some people call themselves the Black Radical Feminists … *I* wanted to be a Black Radical Feminist! I didn't know what that was but … Yes! They were at the front, disrupting the space, occupying it, speaking their mind. *I* wanted to speak my mind, too – but I couldn't find my voice at that point, it was still only a squeak.

BOITSHOKO: We started shifting the furniture around in preparation for our first meeting. I stood against a wall holding a plaque honouring Prof Archie Mafeje, UCT's first black professor.

CAHYA: That day we would become Biko blacks. That day we taught ourselves, as the movement, what we meant when we spoke about white supremacy, institutional racism and black pain at UCT.

CAMILLA: I probably learned more in that eight-hour plenary than I did in my three years at UCT, bra.

The song and dancing build as THE CAST gathers in a circle.

The singing and dancing is interrupted by:

ZUKILE-LIBALELE: One settler …

ALL: One bullet …

ZUKILE-LIBALELE: One bullet …

ALL: One settler …

ZUKILE-LIBALELE: Settler, settler …

ALL: Bullet, bullet …

ZUKILE-LIBALELE: Bullet, bullet …

ALL: Settler, settler …

The song continues. THE CAST settle themselves into their positions for the next scene.

SCENE 2: THE FIRST PLENARY

CAHYA: Izwe lethu …

ALL: iAfrika.

CAHYA: iAfrika …

ALL: Yizwe lethu.

CAHYA: Inkululeko …

ALL: Ngoku.

BOITSHOKO raises his hand. CAHYA steps out; THE CAST freeze as CAHYA speaks directly to the audience.

CAHYA: This movement belongs to all of us. It belongs to a whole lot of groups that worked towards transformation at this university. Like the Trans collective – I'm non-binary, I'm in that – Imbizo, Black Monday, the Black Academic Caucus, the Workers' Union, the SRC (I'm in that too). Chumani, the comrade that threw pota-pota on the statue, was almost at a loss for words about how shit it is for blacks at this university. Throwing some pooh on that statue was one-hundred-percent articulate. It is amazing, really, how everyone got lit over some pota-pota on a statue, but there was some very hard work around transformation long before he did that.

THE CAST unfreeze. Chaos. CAHYA addresses the group:

Cadres please, we need to talk about the statue: Are we going to meet with management or not?

BOITSHOKO still has his hand up.

BOITSHOKO: Chair, I think that we must reject the meeting with management. They don't care about us. All they *ever* do is *talk*. What we need to do is to remove the statue ourselves.

CAHYA: Thank you; captured. Hand there.

KGOTHATSO: Chair, I don't think we should completely reject meeting with management. If we take down that statue ourselves, it will be seen as an act of violence.

ZUKILE-LIBALELE: Cadre, we must be violent with a system that is violent towards us. UFanon teaches us that, ukuthi, 'decolonisation is always a violent phenomenon'. We all know the colonial history of uRhodes; his statue on our campus traumatises us. That man never wanted us to be here.

KGOTHATSO steps out; the rest of the actors freeze as he speaks directly to the audience.

KGOTHATSO: Ya neh, Cecil John Rhodes. I learned about him in my second-year African History course. It was then that I realised that the history they are teaching us is not the history of Africa but rather the history of how Britain and the Superpowers stole Africa and carved it up into little countries, with people like Leopold, Livingstone and Rhodes featuring as heroes. Rhodes didn't only wrap up the Kimberly diamonds for himself and a couple of his buddies – thank you very much – he was an arch imperialist who believed one hundred percent in the superiority of the English Race. All I learned about Africans was how weak we were. Weak in weaponry, tribal in clothing – how we had to be 'civilised' by the great Christian nations. Masepa, what history is that? They say he donated the land, but whose land was it to begin with? Chair …

Lighting changes, THE ACTORS unfreeze and KGOTHATSO re-joins the plenary.

CAHYA: *(To ZUKILE-LIBALELE.)* Cadre, please raise your hand and wait to be recognised next time. *(Points to KGOTHATSO)* Please continue.

KGOTHATSO: Cadres, don't misunderstand me, I am not saying that we must be friendly with management. What I am saying is that we must force them to do the work; we cannot go there ourselves.

CAHYA: Okay, captured.

BOITSHOKO: We have already started to put pressure on management by occupying this space, now we need to get the dates. Management doesn't care about us. They must understand now that we are angry, because we can no longer breathe in this space.

ZUKILE-LIBALELE: All I am saying is that if we are serious about decolonisation, then we must be prepared to take matters into our own hands!

THE FLOOR erupts.

CAHYA: Order. *(To CHWAITA.)* Hand there.

CHWAITA: Hi, everyone. I just want to know what we mean by 'decolonisation'? Does this mean we give back everything that the whites made that we use now? Like mobile phones, clothes, cars, WiFi, this university … Does this mean we have to give up University, now? Banish white people? Go to war?

THE CADRES erupt.

ZUKILE-LIBALELE: My sister, they banished your forefathers. Don't you want to banish them, wena?

CHWAITA: Actually, I am made up of a very wide genealogical range, as are most of you in this room. It's not just about black or white. All I'm just saying is that we must be careful of sounding racist.

THE ENSEMBLE laughs at her and then freezes as she walks to the audience.

CHWAITA: *(To audience.)* I don't know who I am right now, in this space. I mean, I know these people, I know how they perceive me. They think that I don't speak isiXhosa, but I actually do. It is just that people laugh at my accent, so I don't speak it that much. I actually should be back at res., writing my essay. But something's keeping me here and I don't know what it is. These people, this place, this knowledge reminds me of home, of before university, when I still thought I had a voice.

THE ACTORS unfreeze and CHWAITA re-joins the plenary.

CHWAITA: All I'm saying is, we must be careful of our terminology!

CAHYA: Order! Let us stick to the matters at hand and not complicate things.

ZUKILE-LIBALELE raises his hand.

Yes. Hand there.

ZUKILE-LIBALELE: I propose that we bring in a group of people to take down the statue ourselves.

BOITSHOKO: Ya, we mobilise students to come around the statue on the day …

ZUKILE-LIBALELE: Then, we have us, men …

BOITSHOKO: Ya …

ZUKILE-LIBALELE: Bringing a chisel and hammer …

BOITSHOKO: Ya …

KGOTHATSO & CAHYA: A chisel and a hammer? Haihaihai!

BOITSHOKO: Yes! We must do that, cadres!

ZUKILE-LIBALELE: We must use the chisel and a hammer – we all hit it: one, one, one – who are they going to arrest? They can't fit all of us in those vans! Besides, that wouldn't look good on the university.

BOITSHOKO: Ene bona neh, I know someone who has a chisel and a hammer.

Chaos erupts; CAHYA again shushes them.

QHAWEKAZI: Niyadika, man! Cadres, we need to have plans beyond taking down the statue. We can't decolonise with a chisel and a hammer when we were colonised with a Bible and a gun. Think, man, think!

ZUKILE-LIBALELE: Don't undermine us, cadre!

BOITSHOKO: Ya, cadre, don't say we are not thinking.

QHAWEKAZI: But, you're not thinking nje.

BOITSHOKO: Not thinking? Hey, wena, have you seen my marks? Go check my grade book!

CAHYA: Cadres, cadres, cadres, please. We can't afford to fizzle out because of a fight about a chisel and a hammer! I saw the fear on the Vice Chancellor's face today. How is it that he knows our power before we do? What we've done is huge. You're angry; I get it. I'm also angry. I also want to burn this whole place down, but how is that gonna change anything?

ZUKILE-LIBALELE: Chair, with all due respect: Don't talk to us like we are your children, just because you're in the SRC.

CAHYA: It has nothing to do with my position on the SRC and everything to do with your refusal to respect others in this space.

ZUKILE-LIBALELE: We all sacrificed a lot to be here. I still say: the chisel and hammer!

CAHYA: *(To CAMILLA.)* Hand there!

CAMILLA: Okay, so firstly, we have a problem there. That land is a National Heritage site. So you can't just go there, chisel and hammer – qha qha qha! Because you will be arrested and you will be charged. Dololo decolonisation, and you end the whole movement before it even starts. Chair, what we need to do is go to Council –

ZUKILE-LIBALELE: That council full of old racist white men?

KGOTHATSO: Yes, but that council of old white men are the only ones that has the power to decide if the statue stays or goes.

CHWAITA: Why don't we enter the council meeting and force them to make a decision with us there. Nothing about us, without us.

CAHYA: Okay, there's a hand here.

CAMILLA: In the meantime, cadres, we need to discuss other ways of decolonising this institution because we all know it is not just about the statue. I would like to propose a series of lectures and talks with Prof Zethu, Dr Shosi and the Black Academics Caucus …

ZUKILE-LIBALELE: Cadre, you are derailing with these talks and meetings. We need to start talking practically here. When is that colonial statue coming down and how are we bringing it down?

Groans from THE FLOOR.

BOITSHOKO: And we told you, cadres, we know how we are taking it down!

Groans from THE FLOOR.

CAHYA: Don't return to the issue of the chisel and hammer!

BOITSHOKO: Did I say chisel and hammer, cadre!?

ZUKILE-LIBALELE: Okay, chisel and a hammer to the side, ke. I know someone with a truck.

CAHYA & KGOTHATSO: A truck!

THE FLOOR erupts in disbelief.

CAHYA: Order!

ZUKILE-LIBALELE: We just get ropes, tie them on the statue, and pull it down! Just like they did ngoSaddam.

CAMILLA: Cadre, you need to focus. This is not just about the statue! It's about the curriculum. It's about the lack of black lecturers.

KGOTHATSO: It's about how they treat the black workers.

CAMILLA: It's about the art on the walls.

KGOTHATSO: The names on the buildings.

CAMILLA: How we are reflected in this institution.

KGOTHATSO: ... Or not reflected in this institution.

CAMILLA: Exactly!

KGOTHATSO: Chair, we can illuminate issues of why this statue is problematic; through these suggestions rally up the masses, because with the masses it will be easier for us to pressurise management to remove that statue. And it will be a victory for us, not management.

CAHYA: Captured. Hand there.

QHAWEKAZI: I agree with my cadre here. We go to Council, we tell them when, we tell them how to take that statue down. We have the power in this situation.

BOITSHOKO: Sorry, but it still sounds like we're asking permission. Why must we always ask for permission from a white man?

KGOTHATSO: Because they have the power, cadre!

BOITSHOKO: Listen, you cannot carry out fundamental change without a certain amount of madness. In this case, it comes from non-conformity, the courage, cadres, to turn our backs on the old formulas, the courage to invent the future.

ZUKILE-LIBALELE: Injalo, utsho noSankara.

QHAWEKAZI: Safa ngoSankara.

CAHYA: There is a hand there.

CHWAITA: Chair, I am a little bit confused. Didn't management say that they want the statue down; aren't they just following due process?

Laughter from THE FLOOR.

ZUKILE-LIBALELE: Due process? I've followed due process at this university and where has it gotten me? Threats of exclusion. If I am excluded, that means six years of medical school would have been for nothing. I was

22

clinically depressed, cadres, I went to Student Wellness and got all of the correct doctors' notes; I even applied for an extension and handed it in on time. And now, because I missed one week of practicals, this racist lecturer of mine wants to fail me? Due process for who? I say take down that statue soon and we must do it ourselves.

QHAWEKAZI: We sympathise with you, cadre, but we can't take down that statue ourselves.

ZUKILE-LIBALELE: Hey, my sister, don't tell me how to deal with my black pain. Don't come here with your Model C mentality.

CHWAITA: Uh. Wow! Just because you went to a 'Model C School' doesn't mean you don't identify with the cause.

ZUKILE-LIBALELE: Ungqina ntoni ke wena? Yheey, ungqina ntoni?!

He approaches her threateningly; the rest of THE FLOOR goes to stop him.

CAHYA: Order! ORDER!

ZUKILE-LIBALELE: I am sorry, House … Chair … Please can I finish?

CAHYA: You have three seconds.

ZUKILE-LIBALELE: Thank you, Chair. What I am saying is that there are men who are willing to sacrifice everything, including our education. We want to show the world that the fall of Rhodes will be the inevitable fall of white supremacy and privilege on our campus. Can the house please give us the blessings to go do this ourselves?

There is chaos from THE FLOOR.

CAMILLA: Cadre! You would not get halfway through Cecil's blerrie head before they arrested you. Please, some foresight.

BOITSHOKO: Hawu, Camilla, who said we are going to start from the top? We are going to start from the bottom.

ZUKILE-LIBALELE: I want to see Cecil's head rolling down the stairs.

SONG: FROM CAPE TO CAIRO

THE ENSEMBLE sets up tables for the next scene.

SCENE 3: SHARING IN DOWNTIME

THE OCCUPYING STUDENTS relax on the floor with various activities, like playing cards, chatting and sharing anecdotes. While QHAWEKAZI speaks to the audience, BOITSHOKO improvises a dance about being suffocated and having no voice. The dance is in slow motion as are the other activities.

QHAWEKAZI: *(To audience.)* After that, we started talking. Really talking. About our lives, our families, our parents. People started crying, singing and sharing poetry. We had seen each other as strangers on campus many times, not knowing that we were feeling the same suffocation. Craving the same change. I hardly knew anyone in the space, but I felt at home. I remember my mother phoning me, asking about my involvement, because she'd seen me in the news and, of course, I lied to her and told her that I'd only gone for the day to see what was happening. She warned me that I was on financial aid and I couldn't afford to slack behind on my school work, and I agreed – but this space was something new: when we didn't have the words we found new ways to express ourselves.

BOITSHOKO starts dancing in real time. As his dance ends, CAMILLA and KGOTHATSO are playing cards together.

ZUKILE-LIBALELE: Uyazibona ke ezi ze-art.

KGOTHATSO: I want to know. Why am I forever having to prove myself to people who know nothing about my life and what it took to get here?

CAMILLA: I mean, I can guess, but praat maar.

KGOTHATSO: Okay, so I'm trialling for the cricket team.
I wake up at 4.30 am every morning – 4:30! For my
daily runs, I do all my sets without fail, without cutting
corners. Those practice nets at middle campus see my face
every morning as that sun is rising. I've sorted out some
problems with my cut shot, facing spinners, some footwork
issues. I'm dreaming of being the next Themba Bavuma.

CAMILLA: You know, I've seen you there on middle campus,
bra. You kak good.

KGOTHATSO: That comes from my parents; they drummed it
right into me. Work hard and you'll achieve anything you
want. Mara, for what? Only to be told that I don't 'gel'
with the team; the team has good chemistry, so me being a
newcomer might jeopardise that, with Varsity Week round
the corner. I don't make the first team, and bra, I should be
opening that line-up – not even on the bench, tlhe mona.

CAMILLA: This kinda kak discrimination just carries on and
on, round and round; it's not the first time I've heard a
story like this.

KGOTHATSO: And the majority white boys in the team, with
just two – yes – two black players, they all played in league
up north together, or at the coconut Model C schools.
But come from a township like me and they tell you, you
don't gel with the team, because you are the newcomer.
Newcomer! He should have said 'outsider'. We don't know
you. You are not part of the elite, part of the network.

CAMILLA: Is it that white coach?

KGOTHATSO: Ja.

CAMILLA: Now, that's the problem! You know, I've always
wondered what it would feel like to be taught – even
coached – by someone who looks like me. Just a bit of
melanin, please …

KGOTHATSO: That's what I'm saying. All the time. I mean, yissis, look me in the eyes and tell me that I'm not good enough to be in your team. That is a more viable fucking excuse for not allowing another black boy in your team. But don't bullshit me and tell me that I don't gel in well with the team. I mean, go look at my run-rate. It is on the board for everyone to see. Ke masepa afeng ao, what more does the man want from me?

CAMILLA: *(Refers to cards.)* I don't know what he wants, but I want you to play, before I take your money.

KGOTHATSO: Hey, you like money, ne?

CAMILLA: You know mos, asinamali.

ZUKILE-LIBALELE: You know what I want to say to some of my classmates who keep asking to shorten my name? I want to say, you don't understand how disrespectful you are being right now for mispronouncing my name, for misspelling my name, and now you want to shorten it? Do you know when my grandmother gave me my name she had to do a whole praise poem and now you come here and giggle between every syllable? Actually, go learn how to say my name properly, the way I learnt how to say Tchaikovsky and Dostoyevsky.

CHWAITA: What-a-wow! Thank you for actually putting it in words for me. My name is Chwaita, but I have been called Kwaito almost all my life and I just never knew how to …

QHAWEKAZI: You know, the first time I felt othered in this university, was in first-year English class. *(To CAMILLA.)* Ya, you were there! The lecturer was brilliant. The only reason I knew he was brilliant, was because of how much the white kids mmm'd and aaah'd every time he spoke. He kept throwing around these big English words and the only people who could catch them were the white kids and the ones who went to Model C schools.

CHWAITA: I loved him!

QHAWEKAZI: Ugh, she 'loved him'! Dude, the content … It was ridiculous; we read these two problematic books, one after the other. Uhm … *Passage to India* and *Heart of* …

CAHYA: *Heart of Redness.*

CAMILLA: No, that's Zakes Mda.

CHWAITA: *Heart of Darkness* – Joseph Conrad!

QHAWEKAZI: Okay …? Anyway now, if you've read those books you know that black people are portrayed as savages, and the lecturer just throws them at us! No discussion! He doesn't even –

CAHYA: He doesn't even make you critically analyse the Western view of the black body.

QHAWEKAZI: And then, when we finally got to do African Literature, for, like, two – just two – months out of the entire year, the white students sat at the back of the lecture hall and made fun of the African lecturer's accent.

CAHYA: The same thing happened with me in Film and Media.

QHAWEKAZI: One white girl even went as far as saying that black people, by virtue of our melanin, were more suited to working outside in the fields, you know, because, mos, our skin absorbs the heat. Whereas white people, because they have sensitive skin, should be indoors; you know, running things, doing admin. I was like, what the fuck? What century?

CAHYA: Speaking about African lit., I have also written a little something nyana.

QHAWEKAZI: Aich! Wena – Azanian Poet!

CAHYA: You know me, Babes.

CHWAITA & QHAWEKAZI: 'The Town-Ship is sinking'!

CAHYA: Okay, okay! Thank you!

CAHYA performs a poem in slam poetry style. The rest of THE CAST engages in the rhythm and reactions.

I am at the airport. And here you are.

Wrapped in my history, stitched into the fabric of my existence.

Where is Maweni?

Where is my great-grandmother's Tswana?

Where is my great-grandfather's Venda?

Sold into the illusions of apartheid

They let go of their name and adopted you –

This thing.

I realise that there is only one way to rid me of you

Where you have been sneaky

Silent

Small

And like magic have placed yourself within me for 23 years:

You've been a sneaky bitch

The only way to evict you is to do it loudly, publicly, openly

I cannot board my next flight with this baggage

I cannot take flight until I find Maweni

Until I find Ma.

SONG: ELILIZWE.

ZUKILE-LIBALELE: Mna ndingu Zukile Libalele, uGxarha!
uVambane, uMlawu, uCwerha, uSiyoyo, uMahlahlana,

iHlahla elathathwa lajulwa phesheya komlanjana kwathiwa kulo: "Khula hlahla, khula… sogawula kuwe iintonga".

> [My name is Zukile Libalele, a descendent of the Gxarha river, an extension of the Vambane clan, the Mlawus, from uCwerha, uSiyoyo, uMahlahlane – the tree that was tossed over the river and landed on fertile soil, a clan that was called into existence: 'Khula hlahla,' grow, you tree … till you bear us fruits.]

Memory knows our history, yet books fail to recognise it. Clan names paint history right before our eyes in rich images of our sovereign past. Our ancestors … we draw our strength from the Almighty. Heyi mna ndithi ndingu Zukile Libalele, Ahh! uGxarha, uVambane, uMlawu amalawu entwezi, oCwerha, Siyoyo, Mahlahlana. Khula hlahla. Khula, so'gawula kuwe iintonga.

This spills over into a moment of improvised singing and rhythmic drumming on the tables and floor. BOITSHOKO interrupts this.

BOITSHOKO: Hey! Did you guys see the e-mail from UCT …?

CAMILLA: Who – Nadierah Pienaar?

BOITSHOKO: … 'As the University of Cape Town, we are dedicated to transformation …

CHWAITA & QHAWEKAZI: Decolonisation …

BOITSHOKO: Eish, right? 'creating platforms where we can have open discussions about issues of transformation …'

ALL: Decolonisation.

BOITSHOKO: Hebana! '…There will be a mass meeting on the 12th March at 1pm and we invite the UCT community at large to be in attendance.'

CAHYA: This is the meeting they want Barney Pityana to chair.

KGOTHATSO: Who is Barney Pityana?

CAHYA: He was a friend of Steve Biko.

CHWAITA: But he definitely just wrote an article saying Rhodes should stay.

CAHYA: What?!

QHAWEKAZI: Exactly. So he cannot be chairing any meeting at any university right now.

CAHYA: But when they asked the SRC, we said yes, as long as someone from Student Parliament is up there with him.

SONG: PHAMBIRI NGE-CHIMURENGA

QHAWEKAZI: No, we don't care. The SRC cannot be making decisions on behalf of this movement.

CAHYA: Okay, okay. Then we have to go to the meeting and remove him ourselves. Nothing about us, without us. Angithi?

SCENE 4: THE MASS MEETING

THE ACTORS sing 'Phambiri Nge-Chimurenga' and stack the tables in a straight line, with the table tops facing the audience. Visuals of the mass meeting are projected on to the tables behind which THE ACTORS position themselves with tape over their mouths, on which is penned '#RhodesMustFall'. Every time they speak, they remove and then replace the tape over their mouths.

CAHYA: We occupied that meeting. We removed management's biased chairperson and replaced him with a black student. We made sure that for the first half an hour, only those affiliated with the movement spoke.

KGOTHATSO: It was at this mass meeting that people really began to understand what black pain was about, what institutionalised racism was about, and what transformation was needed. People got up, one after another – students, workers, academics – testifying to the invisible racism at UCT.

CHWAITA: This was the first time that black academics got up to speak about their experiences. A highly qualified black lecturer – she had a doctorate – told us how she'd been trying to get a permanent position at the university for six years, but eventually ended up getting a low-rated temporary position at R9 000 per month, just so she could start to teach us.

ZUKILE-LIBALELE: A cleaner got up and spoke about how she was constantly disrespected by white lecturers, and students. How they were made to feel like third-class citizens. You know, cleaning up students' vomit after a rough night at 'Taager-Taager, bru'. I mean, come on.

QHAWEKAZI: For me, the clearest thing was, this guy – I think he said his name is Mohammed – said that institutionalised racism isn't overt, it's what happens between the lines. It's about educated people using rationalisation to negate our lived experience. We will not compromise on our emancipation because it makes you feel uncomfortable.

CAMILLA: Adam Haupt said something that really stuck with me, he said: symbols matter; signifiers matter. But this is just the beginning of the decolonial process. And then this white guy got up, and I can't believe I'm quoting him, but he said: 'It is unacceptable that this many years after apartheid we still have such a disproportionate staff and student body, and it's unacceptable that in an African university the syllabi are still so Eurocentric.'

BOITSHOKO: You know, one thing I don't understand is that even though white people claimed to have removed themselves from their colonial ancestors, for some reason, every time we spoke about the need to remove the statue of Rhodes, they took it as a personal attack. We were saying 'Rhodes Must Fall', not 'whites must fall'.

Singing escalates, then softer again.

CAHYA: These statues, these names, these paintings – none of them represent black excellence. White people don't live in a reality world where white excellence is invisible, where you have to go searching for it. But that world is our reality.

The song rises.

SCENE 5: RHODES FALLS

THE ACTORS arrange the tables to create the plinth where Rhodes's statue once sat and begin toyi-toyiing around it in intense excitement and anticipation. One by one, the performers move forward and address the narrative to the audience. The atmosphere is electric.

'Phambiri!' continues to underscore the speeches.

CAMILLA: I was away when it happened. I went for a research trip to Istanbul and I missed it, but luckily for me, every news agency from around the world was there on my behalf, so I managed to live-stream it. It was supposed to happen at 5pm, but the truck driver was late – you know mos, African time – so I watched the crowd, instead. Hundreds of people pushing against one another; all races, all genders, there to witness history. And I was on the couch of my AirBnB rental in Istanbul. But then, it was finally 5.30.

KGOTHATSO: Something big is about to happen … masses waiting impatiently for him to come down off his colonial throne … We marched up from Bremner (now Azania House) where there were a lot of speeches given by student leaders and black academics. I was getting restless, I wanted it done already. I felt like a Lemon Twist that has just been shaken and is ready to pop and spray. On our way to Upper I swear I could feel the bones of our ancestors moving with us, supporting us in our first step of decolonisation. And now, there he sits, unaware that his time is up. Woza Afrika! Rhodes is falling!

CAHYA: The atmosphere among my fellow comrades is euphoric. We have brought this change, we have forced management to listen to our needs and for the first time, we feel the power, and Rhodes was powerless.

The song rises and ends at the start of BOITSHOKO's monologue. THE ACTORS freeze, looking up at the plinth; they react in slow motion.

BOITSHOKO: At last, the crane lifted the statue, and there was a gasp from the crowd, everything slowed down. Rhodes was suspended in the air and he swung a few inches above the plinth …

THE ACTORS sway slowly. They celebrate their triumph in various slow motion gestures as the statue is removed.

BOITSHOKO: … like he wasn't sure if he should get off, or not. It looked like his ghost was fighting back, trying to make him topple over and crush our black bodies one more time. But he was gone … he was finally gone … I felt as if our land had just heaved a giant sigh of relief; a space to breathe, at last. As the statue landed on the flatbed truck, I saw the look of arrogance on his face. So I jumped on that truck and gave him six lashings with my belt.

THE ACTORS clap their hands six times in unison.

ALL: *(In slow-motion.)* Voertsek!

ZUKILE-LIBALELE: I couldn't help it; I jumped on to the empty plinth and stood up there, tall, dancing. I was painted in black charcoal, my wrist and ankle tied with a silver chain rattling behind me with each step I took, echoing with the sounds of the chains of the enslaved people arriving from the Far East and the African coast, echoing the cries of the Xam clan who were annihilated by the settlers, the displaced Xam Ka !Ke, Khoi, Abathwa, AmaNguni, AmaXhosa, the lost lands, the lost cattle, the lost lives on the mines. I felt like David defeating Goliath, calling out to Azania from Cape to Cairo.

Slow clap starts, initiated by ZUKILE-LIBALELE, with the rest of THE ACTORS following suit.

CHWAITA: When Rhodes fell, the world stopped. History was suspended in the air and continued to wash over us, like a salty, healing wave. UMakana has finally arrived. The earth shook and crumbled. I heard ooMam'Qadi, ooJola, ooDosini scratch at their coffins from underground. I heard the clinking scratch and push of the metal gates. I heard the slaves who hadn't arrived and the singing on the *Mendi*. I heard the cameras buzz. I heard Eric Garner across the Atlantic. The taunts of the people around me, reprimands at the excited crowd – we're foaming at the mouth! I heard the noose pull. The tree branch snap.

THE ACTORS stop clapping.

UNongqawuse is breathing here with us and Solomon's garden is growing.

QHAWEKAZI: I remember looking at the place where the statue had been and I noticed a tiny hole filled with ash and burnt paper. I remember thinking, 'We have to fill that space with *us*.' Things, shapes, people we can recognise. Now the real work of decolonising starts. I remember people looking at us, like, 'Your stupid statue is gone, now you can go back to class; everything is good, you're free.' I suddenly felt too young for this. It felt huge. I remember someone yelling, 'We must replace it with a statue of Tata Nelson Mandela,' and I thought, 'No … we have enough of those, we have enough statues of men. We have enough men.'

As QHAWEKAZI performs this monologue, THE ACTORS re-arrange the tables to set up for the next scene.

SCENE 6: THE PATRIARCHAL 'PLENARY'

QHAWEKAZI: You see, now that Rhodes had fallen, all the problems that the movement had been pushing aside began to come back into focus. The issue of gender had been simmering throughout the occupation and now that the statue was gone, those tensions began to boil over. The radical feminists were demanding that the men account for their patriarchal behaviour, while the men were feeling more and more attacked.

CAMILLA: *(To THE ACTORS.)* Okay, cadres, so when I was in Istanbul all I saw on the live stream were the men. Now, I know that before I left there was a mandate that the women would be put on the frontlines, the women would read statements and the women would interact with the media. Kaanti, no women. So, what happened?

CHWAITA: And let's remember that it was even a problem that we had to be 'put' there in the first place.

KGOTHATSO: But there were women reading the statements at Bremner *and* at the falling of Rhodes!

BOITSHOKO: And we all know that the media favours men. That's the way the world is built. You actually can't blame us here.

CHWAITA: What you guys did was to definitely derail our narrative! By jumping on that plinth, you gave the media this big photo op! We know the media do that. They're not going to focus on these little statements we made as women. The media is only interested in the dramatic picture, so when you jumped on that plinth, you immediately elevated yourselves. Now, ding! This picture is all over social media, all over the news, looking like you are the leaders of this movement.

CAMILLA: And on top of that, cadre, you should've heard what those European journalists were saying about you.

You know, the minute he pulled out his belt and started hitting Cecil in the face, they called him a savage.

KGOTHATSO: Why do we care about what the Europeans think of us?

CHWAITA: Uh, we definitely have to think about the global perception of this movement.

BOITSHOKO: But what was wrong with it? You could have easily jumped on the statue if you wanted to.

CHWAITA: But you guys are constantly changing the terms! I don't want to have to compete with you for the spotlight by becoming hyper-masculine and jumping on flatbed trucks and hitting statues. Just stick to the plans! We had an agreement!

BOITSHOKO: So, are you saying now that I can't express myself naturally? This is biology, not hyper-masculinity. When we are in spaces like that, testosterone takes over. What must happen? *(Gestures rather aggressively.)*

QHAWEKAZI: Cadre, this is the hyper-masculinity they keep telling you about. Check thyself, please.

CAHYA: And people must not speak of biology when they don't know the implications. We have spent hours here defining hyper-masculinity to you and telling you how violent that behaviour is to other cadres in the space.

CAMILLA: Ja, must we now sit in fear because your testosterone could kick in at any minute?

KGOTHATSO: But, that's completely different.

CAMILLA: How?

KGOTHATSO: What happened last week was a historic moment in our lives. You are our queens! We love you. We are the head and you are the neck. You are our support! That is the African way.

CAHYA: Can I remind you that there are not just cis-het people in this space? It is not just man-woman, man-woman.

QHAWEKAZI: I have been telling you, these men are never gonna get it.

KGOTHATSO: Then teach us, please. I am getting defeated now.

CAMILLA: Teach you?

BOITSHOKO: Yes, please, guys! You're stressing me out.

CAMILLA: It's not my job to teach you how you oppress me. The same way it's not your job to teach a white man how he oppresses you.

BOITSHOKO: Baby girl, I was born in the township, ke tswa kokasi, and until I came here, I have never heard of these feminist ideas …

CAMILLA: It's not about coming from ekasi, bra. You're here now, you've got eduroam. Just go do a young Google search, go look up Phumla Gqola and Panashe Chigumadze and educate yourself! I am not your fucking teacher! I mos don't get paid a teacher's salary; it's not right.

KGOTHATSO: Cadre, so how are you expecting us to act? Are you saying that all men from kokasi are 'hyper-masculine' and 'patriarchal'?

CAMILLA: It is the mentality that 'male bodies are the heads and female bodies are the necks' that is contributing to the rape culture in this country.

KGOTHATSO: Whoa, whoa! Just because I'm a black man from kokasi, I'm a rapist?

CAMILLA: That's not what I'm saying, cadre, and you know it's not what I'm saying.

CHWAITA: Whoa, cadre, please check yourself.

KGOTHATSO: Then, what?

CAMILLA: I don't give a fuck where you come from! You could come from Bishopscourt, or ekasi or the blerrie moon for all I care! Every man is a potential rapist, until he proves otherwise.

ZUKILE-LIBALELE: Exactly: *potential* rapist! And has anyone been raped in the movement?

Silence.

CAMILLA: Not yet.

QHAWEKAZI: Cadres, the fact that we can afford to sit here and argue about patriarchy verses feminism shows that we think we are very privileged!

CAMILLA: Wow.

QHAWEKAZI: No, I'm sorry, cadres, but there are students in this university who are counting on us to decolonise …

CHWAITA: But that's what we're doing, mos!

QHAWEKAZI: No, we're sitting here arguing.

BOITSHOKO: Mmmmm, thank you, cadre!

QHAWEKAZI: *(Addresses BOITSHOKO.)* Ha-uh, I am not on your side wena! *(Back to the others.)* Cadres, it is very clear that you can't get these men to do what you want. If you can't agree on anything, I propose we do what we came here to do in the first place. Decolonisation, qha!

CAHYA: That is bullshit! Our mission statement clearly states that we are an intersectional movement! These men choose to be ignorant. They must unlearn their patriarchy! I will not be a part of a movement that wants to decolonise this university, and replace it with an African patriarchy.

ZUKILE-LIBALELE: Yheey, yhey yhey wena – don't come here and insult my culture with your white feminist theories.

I am a man, mna. A Xhosa African man. I belong to my culture before my manhood. You may not respect me, but you will respect my culture; so will this institution and everyone here, niyandiva?

CAMILLA: Cadre, all I'm saying is stop selecting parts of African culture that only benefit the men. We blacks have the opportunity here to choose what empowers us and oppresses us.

ZUKILE-LIBALELE: Blacks? *(Laughs.)* Come on now, my sister! We all know coloureds have always had it better.

KGOTHATSO: Whoa, whoa, Zuki, slow down.

ZUKILE-LIBALELE: Hayi, I won't slow down, man. Coloureds can never really understand the depth of black pain. They have white blood in them and now they think they are better than us.

CAMILLA: So, I'm black when I agree with you, and then soema white when I don't?

BOITSHOKO: No, that's not what he meant.

CAMILLA: So what 'n fok does he mean?

BOITSHOKO: He just means that we've got different struggles.

ZUKILE-LIBALELE: Don't tell me what I mean, wena, I know what I mean. Blackness is a lived experience. Not a sub-scription.

CAMILLA: Cadre, you don't 'n fok know me. I come from the Cape Flats, bra; there are girls in my neighbourhood being raped and murdered as gang initiations, so don't tell me I've got it better or easier. My struggle doesn't end with being black. I'm also a queer woman and don't you fokken forget that. Yous are jas if you think this movement is going anywhere with this cis-hetero-patriarchal-pureblood-blackness kak-gedagtes. *(CAMILLA exits.)* Nee, voertsek, julle varke! Skommelaars!

Silence.

CAHYA: Every time we have these discussions about gender you cis-het men and women make it all about you, and the rest of us are sitting here – suffocating. You continue to use these 'he/she', 'brother/sister' binaries even after non-binary cadres have expressed our pain at being referred to under these binaries. You ignore queers, non-binary and transgendered cadres in the space. When you asked us violent and offensive questions, we spent hours here, educating you, trying to validate our existence. We have put our bodies on the line over and over for this movement, but we are still seen as invisible members of this space. Respect us. Respect our existence. You black feminists are Patriarchy Princesses! You refuse to put your money where your mouth is and leave this movement.

CAHYA exits. Silence.

SONG: SHIWELELE

THE CAST resets the tables.

SCENE 7: IN BETWEEN

QHAWEKAZI: Days passed before some of us met again; in the meantime, we found ourselves evicted from Azania 1, without a space to think, talk, laugh and just be black. On one hand, I was glad that we'd had our big separation; it gave us time to deal with underlying issues within the movement.

KGOTHATSO: During the last days of our stay at Azania 1, we were sent an interdict, with four named respondents. In solidarity, we all wrote our names down. We got interdicted too.

QHAWEKAZI: It became clear that the world would not wait for us to find a new space where we could reconcile and finally understand what we meant by intersectionality.

Because, suddenly, another inferno erupted. African nationals living in South Africa began to be attacked and killed.

CAHYA: I returned to the movement when I heard about the peaceful protest at parliament. The Afrophobia issue really got to me and I wanted to support #AfrophobiaMustFall by standing in solidarity with my fellow Africans who were under attack in KZN.

BOITSHOKO: We were calling for our government to account for their slow reaction to the attacks over there. Little did we know that this was only the beginning.

QHAWEKAZI: That day, for the first time, I witnessed how little our lives mattered as black people. I couldn't even begin to imagine how much less valuable a black foreigner's life must be to our government.

ZUKILE-LIBALELE: At parliament we were met with the very same thing we were standing up against: sheer violence. The police man-handled us and detonated stun grenades to disperse the small crowd.

THE ACTORS sit on the floor while the footage from the #AfrophobiaMustFall protest at parliament plays on the wall behind them.

CHWAITA: We moved into Azania 2. We got kicked out of Azania 2. We moved into Azania Hall. We had more talks and seminars. We fought. Some of us lost close white friends, who couldn't understand the need for decolonisation. They kept saying that they shouldn't be held accountable for a history they weren't part of. That we were racists.

BOITSHOKO: We stopped mobilising for a while. Then there was the beginning of everything.

The singing stops.

CAHYA: The next big issue to occupy the movement was the #EndOutsourcing campaign.

CHWAITA: The workers had been supporting us the entire year. So now it was our turn to do the same for them.

BOITSHOKO: It started with Down Tools. All the workers at UCT were encouraged to boycott work on that day and join a mass march and meeting at Jameson Hall, which we renamed Marikana Memorial Hall.

ZUKILE-LIBALELE: There, the workers once again voiced their ill-treatment at work, the injustices of outsourcing.

CAHYA: And then, another wave.

ALL: Wits!

SONG: SOLOMONI

SCENE 8: FEES MUST FALL

THE ACTORS move into a semi-circle around the stage, with CAMILLA re-joining them. The atmosphere is one of excitement and action.

CAHYA: It was announced that fees would increase the next year by nearly 12%. This ignited students countrywide. Wits students began occupying an admin building that they renamed Solomon Mahlangu House. Social media was ablaze with hashtag 'National Shut Down'. But here at UCT, we decided that we would not let the fees issue overshadow outsourcing. The two would go forward hand-in-hand.

KGOTHATSO: The first barricades went up that Monday, here on campus. We used bins and large rocks. The workers had their jobs on the line and could not actively go on strike, so we had to do rounds to fetch them from their posts.

CHWAITA: I remember coming home from drama class that evening when I heard there was a gathering outside Bremner. Our comrades at Wits had warned us about teargas and stun grenades, so my friends and I went prepared with water bottles and T-shirts to use as protection. Shit got real when a hippo screeched in and stopped right in front of us. This was the first time on campus that the police began to tear gas us and stun grenade people.

ZUKILE-LIBALELE: The next day barricading continued. Some of us marched around campus mobilising and releasing workers, while others continued to barricade – Hiddingh, Middle Campus, Business School, College of Music, Dance School, everywhere, bra.

CAMILLA: That day, the police came to the barricades I was at, and started arresting students. They put them in these headlocks and threw them into the back of their vans, taking them God knows where. Now, I had returned to the movement because I wanted to support Fees Must Fall. As hurt as I was, I believed one hundred percent in free education. You see, I was going to graduate at the end of the year with a NSFAS loan of over R100 000, and I don't have the kind of money to pay that back. So much for the Freedom Charter and Bill of Rights, promising us free education. Gha.

THE ACTORS have arranged the tables straight across the stage as if for a large press conference. They sit on top of the tables. Lighting change, the song stops.

ZUKILE-LIBALELE: Bill of Rights, Section 28: *'Everyone has the right to further education which the state through reasonable measures must make progressively available and accessible.'* In Section 8 of the Freedom Charter it was agreed:

'The Doors of Learning and of Culture shall be opened! Education shall be free, compulsory, universal and equal for all children. Higher education and technical training shall be opened to all by means of state allowances and scholarships awarded on the basis of merit.'

QHAWEKAZI: 'Merithi'? How is that even possible? Black people are always a step behind. We are born into this poverty and we are kept there as a way to control us. Instead of the government trying to right the wrongs of the past, we are given loans that are designed to keep us dependent on the system. The very same system that we are fighting against! If you are a university student, you go to the financial aid offices; once you are there, you have to prove just how poor you are. If they don't subscribe to your brand of poverty, then you're fucked. You sit there, putting all of your family's shame and hardships on display, just so you can get a pat on the shoulder that says, 'Congratulations, you're poor enough to qualify for a financial aid loan.'

BOITSHOKO: Well, I'm one of those people who are 'poor enough' to get a full NSFAS loan. From my monthly food allowance, I have to send money home to help pay for my siblings' school fees. After I graduate, I will end up with a huge debt hanging over me. How am I supposed to continue helping my family? I'm not even sure if I'm gonna get a job.

KGOTHATSO: Now, I fall into the 'missing middle'. To NSFAS it seems like I can afford to pay university fees, but it's just not enough, so I end up with less financing and have to find the rest of the money myself. Come from a single-parent household, supporting three children and an extended family … So, now I'm out here stressing about financial exclusion – I'm already behind on last year's payments, and if I don't find the money now, I can't come back next year. Now, imagine if the fees increase! Yho! I'm in deep shit.

ALL: Yoh, reality, tata!

CAHYA: I also come from a single-parent home and fall into the missing middle. After all my bursaries and loans have been deducted from my account, my mother is barely able to pay the R14 000 family contribution. So, I work part-

44

time at a bar to help out. Right now, I'm surviving off of Chinese ginger tea and 2-minute noodles. If fees don't fall, I don't know whether to give up the tea or the noodles.

CHWAITA: Well I'm not a poor student, you know mos, but I've seen what the financial struggle does to my comrades. I've seen my cadre over here – he barely eats! I can't even fathom having to send my *allowance* home, just to help! And I've looked it up, nè. If, say, you're in the sciences and you're clever enough, you may even get a full bursary. But if you're in the humanities, you can forget about it – you're definitely, definitely going to have to carry a financial burden. I mean, why is studying what you love such a debt sentence for black students?

ZUKILE-LIBALELE: Hayi, I still remember, in first year, arriving at Smuts Residence with only R200 for umphako. That's what my family managed to send me off with. Now, for Orientation Week you need close to R1 200 for all the activities they take you on. Where was I going to get that money? So, every day I used to lock myself up in my room and not go to the food hall so that no one would notice that I wasn't joining them on the field trips. With each day that came to pass, the privilege of white students became more apparent to me.

BOITSHOKO: That is why we demand free, decolonised education in our lifetime! Sithi phantsi nge-Fees phantsi!

ALL: Phantsi!

SONG: SIZONGENA NGE-SOCIALISM

The tables are rearranged to create the gates of parliament. THE ACTORS once more assemble around it in a muted form of a toyi-toyi as the song underscores the following:

CAHYA: On Wednesday the call went out to march on parliament while they were in session. We wanted Blade Nzimande to hear our demands. The call had gone from a call for no fee increase, to no fees at all. But we didn't know how we would get there, so, in a fit of frustration, some of the Jammie drivers went rogue and decided to drive us to parliament themselves. But listen to this: the police stopped us halfway with tazers and pepper spray, so we walked the rest of the way.

CAMILLA: I went to Hiddingh campus to pick up the cadres who were there. We were all very ready to get to parliament, and then – believe it or not – we were sent ten pizzas from the Italian restaurant across the road, *Nonna Lina*. So, of course, we were a little late to parliament, like soz [sorry].

ZUKILE-LIBALELE: We were the first to get to parliament, but the moment we arrived, up went the danger tape, and all of a sudden, police started milling around.

BOITSHOKO: Things stayed calm for a while, until CPUT students arrived and burnt a tyre right outside parliament! And then, all of a sudden, there was singing and the crowd grew as UWC students arrived; more workers, Stellenbosch students, more UCT students, and, of course, journalists.

THE ACTORS move towards BOITSHOKO, creating a tight group around him.

BOITSHOKO: The police started putting on their riot gear. And we thought, oh shit, this is getting real.

CAMILLA: We walked through Company Gardens with the pizzas and some water. It was bloody hot and cadres needed refreshment.

ZUKILE-LIBALELE: I was standing just behind a group of people who were beginning to seriously get lit. They were pushing and shoving and battering at the big double iron gates to parliament. Suddenly, zakadla! A tsunami mfondini.

THE ACTORS create a wave of bodies and fall on to the ground.

KGOTHATSO: We did not open those gates! I swear we did not force them. They opened those gates for us. They invited us in. So in we went! The police were quick. They went between us and the doors to parliament. As more people poured in, we shouted:

ALL: We want Blade! Give us Blade!

KGOTHATSO: Our demand was for free education, free access for all! We were done compromising. Too expensive, plus no increase, still equals too expensive! Izwe lethu!

ALL: iAfrika!

KGOTHATSO: iAfrika!

ALL: Izwe lethu!

KGOTHATSO: Inkululeko!

ALL: Ngoku!

CHWAITA: The police began warning us and hitting us with their riot shields. All of the students at the front were black and so a call was made for our white allies to form a human shield around us. And I remember a policeman telling a white girl that they didn't want to hurt them and I thought, ja, you see, nothing has changed.

A protest song of Hah! Hah! (repeated) starts as THE ACTORS toyi-toyi.

CAMILLA: So, there we were, walking down Government Avenue, with the pizzas. We had just passed the Iziko National Gallery when we heard this befokte groot bang.

ZUKILE-LIBALELE bangs his hands on the table. The singing stops briefly, then picks up slowly.

CAMILLA: And then, silence. And then, three more.

ZUKILE-LIBALELE bangs his hands three times on the table. THE ACTORS disperse in reaction to the stun grenades. Footage of the march to parliament is projected on to the entire stage and back wall as the story continues.

47

QHAWEKAZI: The first stun grenade was aimed over the line of white kids into the black students and workers behind them. We dispersed briefly and when we returned, the white kids went to the front again, daring the police to arrest them. They threw three stun grenades and then more and more. We dispersed again, this time running back into Government Avenue.

CAMILLA: We arrived just in time to see the gates of parliament closing. Now there was a group inside parliament gardens, and another group outside, trying to get back in.

CAHYA: On my way out, my phone fell. I bent down to pick it up, and I was trapped inside. I looked down and all I saw was sunglasses and flip-flops. Now, sunglasses I get, but who the hell protests in flip-flops?

QHAWEKAZI: I followed the crowd out, looking for my friends, when I tripped and fell. A white guy picked me up and I thought … This is the South Africa Nelson Mandela dreamed of: where black and white protest together and pick each other up.

ZUKILE-LIBALELE: The chaos continued and they kept stun-grenading and we kept dispersing and coming back. I remember a policeman getting hit with his own helmet. They were our fathers, but we were fighting on opposite ends.

QHAWEKAZI: Nank'ya u-Blade!

ALL: *(Ad lib. In variation)* Phi?! Yhey, voertsek wena, phuma apho!

CAHYA: Blade eventually came out, after three hours in the sun, without a mic or even a loud-hailer. Rha! He was disrespecting us. Respect us!

ALL: *(Ad lib.)*

ZUKILE-LIBALELE: I couldn't even see Blade. I just kept hearing people saying that he was standing on a balcony, with no one hearing him.

BOITSHOKO: I was standing right in front of that balcony. I saw him. I was one of the first people to throw my water bottle at him. I was so pissed, bra. We were all fucking pissed. Blade went back in and the police started shoving us out.

KGOTHATSO: They blocked all the streets, leaving only Roeland Street to get out. We were chased; they hunted us.

CHWAITA: The police vans were blocking taxis, so I went in search of my friends. I needed them.

CAMILLA: Some students had to be taken to hospital to get their wounds dressed; they had second-degree burns from a stun grenade.

KGOTHATSO: I just needed a drink, so we went to the Pig and Swizzle.

CAMILLA: My mom phoned me when I got back to res., and she warned me: first comes the stun grenades, then come the water cannons, then come the bullets. I wondered who among us would be the first to die.

SONG: THINA SIZWE

THE ACTORS remain still as the projections of the protest at parliament plays behind them.

QHAWEKAZI: I was still pissed, man. We left the same way we came. We got no answers, only disrespect and violence. After parliament, the government decided that they were not going to raise the fees, and people were celebrating. Why the fuck were they celebrating? It's not like we could afford the fees before!

CAHYA: Meanwhile, it was decided by the movement that shutdown would continue and no one would write their

final exams until management agreed to insource all
outsourced workers.

ZUKILE-LIBALELE: I sympathised with the workers, but
cancellation of our upcoming exams is a very big problem
for me. I mean, I love the movement. As a Health Sciences
student, they have helped me fight my unfair treatment
and I appreciate that. I got to learn a lot of things through
the movement, not only about the oppression of the
institutions, but also about myself. It wasn't only whiteness
that felt the pressure, kodwa nathi black men were under a
lot of scrutiny. My anger was constantly checked and as a
cultural man, I often felt misunderstood and disrespected.
I got so angry, eventually I stopped going to plenaries for
a while. And that's when I felt like I needed my faith the
most.

The song ends.

ZUKILE-LIBALELE: But then again, Christianity was criticised
a lot in the movement and I was left rather confused
and feeling hurt. However, through consistent talks and
engagements with the men and women – or maybe
I should say cis-het men and women, because I am
beginning to understand these terms – that's when I got
back to myself. That's when I remembered my God-given
purpose, which is to serve the people, the sick. In fact, that
is what has brought me back here.

SCENE 9: MEDICAL PLENARY

*THE STUDENTS are gathered for a crucial plenary in which the medical
students are asking for permission to break the shutdown by doing their
final exams. The atmosphere is unsettled, tense and noisy.*

QHAWEKAZI: Cadres, cadres, please. All the Health Sciences
students ask is that we hear them out; please cadres, some
patience. Continue.

ZUKILE-LIBALELE: Cadres, I understand we are not special,
but we all cannot stand and sit here in the comfort of UCT

and deny what is impoverishing our people ekasi – it is sicknesses and diseases like HIV, TB, diabetes. In fact, some cadres are not with us today because they have to look after a sick person at home. We are being trained to serve those people. Can the house please allow us to complete our exams?

QHAWEKAZI: Thank you; captured, cadre.

BOITSHOKO: Cadres, how many times have we had to yield to white power? How many times have we had to yield to the system? Hey, my brother, you're the same person who wanted us to take matters into our own hands and remove the statue ourselves. Now you come here and accuse us of being counter-revolutionary when you want to go back into the system, the very same system that stun-grenaded us last week. Don't come here with your sell-out tendencies.

QHAWEKAZI: Thank you; name calling, please.

CAHYA: Chair, I sympathise with our cadre over here, but if we let the Health Sciences students write, we will have every other faculty here, standing at our door, requesting to write exams. Heh-eh, most of us have already accepted the fact that we are repeating another year.

KGOTHATSO: Are you saying our mothers must die in hospital!? Ha-uh.

CAHYA: That's not what I'm saying!

BOITSHOKO: I am saying, if people die and someone asks why, we must tell them the government didn't give us fees for education.

QHAWEKAZI: Okay, thank you. Hand.

CHWAITA: Chair, I know we're saying fuck the system, but we can't push ourselves to this extent – of being willing to harm innocent people! We're talking about people's lives here.

BOITSHOKO: No! Business can't continue as usual, we have to involve the public sector.

KGOTHATSO: No, no, no, cadre –

BOITSHOKO: In a revolution there are casualties, sacrifices!

KGOTHATSO: So, you want people to die! Chair! Chair!

BOITSHOKO: The government will see that we are willing to risk.

QHAWEKAZI: Cadres, please! Yes, Camilla.

CAMILLA: Chair, I just want to know why the medical students think they are so special that they are the only ones going out into the public sector. What about the teachers and the lawyers? If we let them finish, then we must let everyone finish.

CHWAITA: Chair, I feel like this cadre is completely derailing this whole thing …

CAMILLA: How?

CHWAITA: We are not talking about teachers, we are not talking about lawyers. These are medics. In fact, I need to call you to order, cadre, because what you are inciting, is black-on-black violence.

CAMILLA: Me?

CHWAITA: Yes, you, cadre!

KGOTHATSO: Cadres, we can't make ourselves judge and jury over people's lives! We are all dealing with lives in this movement. Everything will be affected in this movement!

BOITSHOKO: What needs to be done, needs to be done.

ZUKILE-LIBALELE: Cadres, I remember, even uPastor Skhosana said we must serve within the positions we are given. We are Health Sciences students. That is our contribution. That is what we do, something we have always done for this movement. Allow us to write these final exams.

CAMILLA: Chair, he's going in circles here!

THE STUDENTS become unruly, speaking over one another.

QHAWEKAZI: High morale.

ALL: High discipline.

QHAWEKAZI: High discipline.

ALL: High morale.

QHAWEKAZI: Cadres, I understand everyone is on edge, but I have said already this is a very sensitive topic. We cannot afford to be rushing over such decisions.

ZUKILE-LIBALELE: The way you are speaking scares me. There is a whole class of health workers waiting to graduate into the health system. If we do not write our exams, you are denying our people our services. This is one way that can literally kill black people. Not the mental way – that we have been enslaved – but literally, kill black people.

CAMILLA: Chair, let me please just remind the house that the point of the shutdown is to put pressure on government and universities to give us funds for free education and insourcing of workers. The same workers who are sitting here listening to us argue. Cadres, we all agreed that the Health Sciences students would be pressure points for government.

ZUKILE-LIBALELE: Pressure points? Cadres, you can't use us Health Sciences as political leverage.

KGOTHATSO: The system has always used black lives as political leverage. Please reconsider!

THE STUDENTS erupt in disagreement.

CHWAITA: Chair! I didn't want to say this, but cadres, you leave me no option. All of you are a bunch of fucking hypocrites! If everything must shut down, then financial aid office must also shutdown.

CAHYA: Chair, I would like to request that we all get an exam pad, nè? We write down all our account details, so her father can pay our allowances!

Eruption.

KGOTHATSO: Shut down the medical campus; go ahead, shut it all down, but please let them complete their exams!

CAMILLA: Cadres, shut down means shut down! Every building must be closed! The wellness centre, the reses, the financial aid office. Even the toilets must shut down!

BOITSHOKO: The shit must overflow in the toilets!

CAHYA: Yes! The HOD's must clean it themselves!

BOITSHOKO: Yes! This is war!

KGOTHATSO: War, cadre? War?! Do you have no rules when it comes to war? Hospitals, churches, schools – these are neutral zones in a war, cadre.

QHAWEKAZI: Okay, cadres, like I mentioned before, this is not an easy decision to make. I don't know if cadres in this movement know, but the Health Sciences' exams happen in actual hospitals, with real patients. So, unless there are cadres in this movement willing to march into a hospital and physically remove black patients from getting help, there's not much we can do. What I will say is this: *(To ZUKILE-LIBALELE.)* If you decide to continue with your exams, you have to make a noise, something must be done to show management that things are dire out here. You cannot afford to be silent. I know we are angry, but we are a movement of liberated thinkers; we are not a death squad.

SONG: ILANGA.

SCENE 10: SHACKVILLE AND THE FIRST FLAMES

The tables are moved to the back of the stage, upright with their tops facing towards the audience. THE ACTORS place themselves between the tables. QHAWEKAZI moves to the front of the stage.

QHAWEKAZI: No 22-year-old should have to make the call that I just made. Throughout that year I had been hopeful that if black people came together, peacefully, and claimed their stake in this university in a non-violent way, we would be just fine. But after watching us put our humanity on the line like that, I realised that the cycle would never end. A few months later, in the new year, Shackville happened. The university residences were full and many black first-year students were homeless. In protest, we erected a shack on campus.

The footage of Shackville is projected on top of them.

BOITSHOKO: We stormed a nearby dining-hall and started dishing food for ourselves. That's when the paintings started coming off the walls. Paintings that were violent and offensive to us as Black people. We were enraged. Nothing had changed and nothing was improving.

ZUKILE-LIBALELE: I was in Khayelitsha assisting at a local clinic when it happened, so I saw it on Facebook. It was powerful. It was time that the world saw the dire circumstances that most of us come from.

CAMILLA: I couldn't believe that I was watching paintings being burnt. The flames ignited images of a lesbian hate crime, of necklacing foreign nationals, of Nazi Germany. Burning things that we don't like? Is that really where we've come to?

CAHYA: I wanted to burn things, too, but I began fearing for our future. I stood there, frozen, watching those paintings burn, and I did nothing to stop it.

CHWAITA: I'm an artist, but I couldn't judge. I've seen displacement. I've seen the rage of being denied access, of being secondary, of having to defend yourself, your culture, your representation.

THE ACTORS all walk forward to stand in a tight group. The singing stops.

KGOTHATSO: All you see around these walls are white faces. The curriculum promotes white excellence, and anything you do as a black body is just not good enough. That's how racism works. It undoes you, thought by thought, doubt by doubt, and slowly your self-belief crumbles. That is what happened to me when that coach told me I didn't 'gel' with his team. But the movement helped me. Someone sent me a link to a cricket foundation that provides coaches to township schools. That is what I'm doing now, just to keep sane, to give those kids a fighting chance.

BOITSHOKO: I have one regret – I just wish I had contributed more intellectually to the movement, because it is only now that I realise what I am capable of.

CAHYA: I dream of a future where people, even in the smallest of townships, are able to openly live their gender and sexuality without any fear.

ZUKILE-LIBALELE: I truly believe that we can create a system that is inclusive and intersectional, because, more than anything, I believe in the human spirit. We have endured so much already. Sometimes, I get glimpses of it and I am hopeful.

CHWAITA: But that hope can only come once we honestly re-look at the systems that are in place. And once we acknowledge that privilege is not only material – it comes in many forms.

CAMILLA: And, ya, it is going to be tough, but we have to start somewhere. We need to be able to give up certain things. We need to be able to say, just because I'm not in pain, doesn't mean you can't be. Please, let's just have the conversation.

SONG: UYI-NGWE.

THE ACTORS walk on the spot in a tight group as QHAWEKAZI moves forward to deliver her final monologue.

QHAWEKAZI: We used to be people. We used to dream about a future where we didn't need to protest anymore, or call ourselves brave and fearless. There are reasons we call ourselves that. There are reasons some of us are losing our humanity, one protest at a time. There are reasons the workers have gone on strike, reasons black students get angry and it feels like the rest of this country is doing everything in its power to not see them. What do we need to do to show people that we can't keep living like this? To show people that the state of our lives is not normal? That poverty is not normal. The townships we are born into are not normal and we don't want to be forced to be brave anymore. I don't want to be this person. I don't want my life to be a series of violent gatherings, forever running away from the police and their stun grenades. I want to be seen. I want to matter. I'm tired. My soul is tired, but the reasons I came the first time won't let me leave. They won't let me live a normal life.

QHAWEKAZI joins the rest of THE ACTORS in the song and slow run. As they look into the uncertain future, fade to black.

THE END

LYRIC SHEET

SONG: NOBODY WANNA SEE US TOGETHER

CALL: Nobody wanna see us together

RESPONSE: Zumba Zumba yo ayo ayo a zumba zumba yo

CALL: Nobody nobody nobody

RESPONSE: Zumba Zumba yo ayo ayo a zumba zumba yo

CALL: Bazothina bantu bazothina bantu

RESPONSE: Zumba Zumba yo ayo ayo a zumba zumba yo

SONG: MAGWALA A CHE CHE

CALL: Tlosang magwala a che che

RESPONSE: Magwala a che che

A che che le moraho

Hoy a rona ba pelo tse thata ko pele

SONG: BAZOSIBONA THINA

CALL: Bazosibona thina

They will see us

RESPONSE: Aha haaaa

CALL: Bazosibona

They will see us

RESPONSE: Aha haaaa

CALL: Bazosibona thina

RESPONSE: Aha haaaa

CALL: Bazosibona

RESPONSE: Aha ha!

SONG: FROM CAPE TO CAIRO

CALL: iAzania lizwe lethu

Azania is our land

RESPONSE: Azania

CALL: Solithatha nge-Bazooka

We will take it with a gun

RESPONSE: Azania

CALL: From Cape to Cairo

RESPONSE: Azania

CALL: Morocco to Madagascar

RESPONSE: Azania

SONG: ILIWE LOO-KHOKHO BETHU

CALL: Sizabalaz' elilizwe loo-khokho bethu

We are fighting for this land of our great-grandparents

RESPONSE: Sizabalaz' elilizwe

CALL: Sizabalaz' elilizwe labant' abanyama

We are fighting for the land of the blacks

RESPONSE: Sizabalaz' elilizwe

CALL: Elilizwe loo-khokho bethu

RESPONSE: Sizabalaz' elilizwe

CALL: Elilizwe laban' abamnyama

SONG: PHAMBIRI NGECHIMURENGA

CALL: Phambiri nge hondo

Forward with the war

Phambiri nge Chimurenga

Forward with the liberation

Phambiri nge hondo

Phambiri nge Chimurenga

SONG: SHIWELELE

CALL: Shiwelele

RESPONSE: Ho-ah ho ho

CALL: Shiwelele le

RESPONSE: Shiwelele

CALL: Shiwelele lele

RESPONSE: Ho-ah

CALL: Ho-ah-ho

RESPONSE: Ho-ooh.

SONG: SOLOMONI

CALL: Solomoni!

RESPONSE: iYho Solomoni! *(three times)*

CALL: Wayeli soja

      He was a soldier

RESPONSE: iSoja loMkhonto weSizwe

      A soldier for Mkhonto weSizwe

CALL: Elabulawa

      Who was killed

RESPONSE: Ngamabhulu e-Afrika

      By the boers in Africa

SONG: SIZONGENA NGESOCIALISIM

CALL: Sizongena ngeSocialism

      We will proceed with socialism

RESPONSE: Aroba roba roba

      Arube rube rube

CALL: Rube rube rube

RESPONSE: Aroba roba roba

      Arube rube rube

SONG: THINA SIZWE

CALL: Thina Sizwe

We the nation

RESPONSE: Thina Sizwe, esimnyama

We the nation of blacks

CALL: Sikalela

We are crying for

RESPONSE: Sikalela, izwe lethu

We are crying for our land

CALL: Elathathwa

That was taken

RESPONSE: Elathathwa, ngamaburu

That was taken by the boers

CALL: Mababethwe

They should be hit

RESPONSE: Mababethwe bazoyek'umhlaba wethu

They should be so that they leave our land alone

CALL: Mababethwe

RESPONSE: Mababethwe bazoyek'umhlaba wethu

SONG: I-LANGA

CALL: I-langa

The sun

RESPONSE: I-langa xa lishona bazo' buyel' emakhaya

They will go back to their homes when the sun sets

SONG: UYINGWE

CALL: Mfundi uyingwe

   Student, you are a leopard

RESPONSE: Uyingwe, uyingw'esa dubul' isabham'

   You are a leopard shooting a gun

CALL: Satsho kamnandi

   The shots sound comforting

RESPONSE: Uyingw'esa dubul' isabham'